The Boston Tea Party

US History for Kids
Children's American History

BABY PROFESSOR
EDUCATION KIDS

Speedy Publishing LLC

40 E. Main St. #1156

Newark, DE 19711

www.speedypublishing.com

Copyright 2017

The Boston Tea Party occurred on December 16, 1773. It was one of the major events that resulted in the American Revolution.

It was initially referred to as "the Destruction of Tea in America" by John Adams and was a political protest occurring on December 16, 1773 in Boston by a group known as the Sons of Liberty. These demonstrators, some costumed as Mohawk Indians were protesting against the Tea Act. They destroyed a shipment of tea received from the East India Company.

Was It A Big, Fun Party?

No, not really. While tea was involved, no one was drinking it. It was a protest against British government by American Colonists. The protest began by boarding three ships in the Boston Harbor and throwing their tea cargo into the ocean.

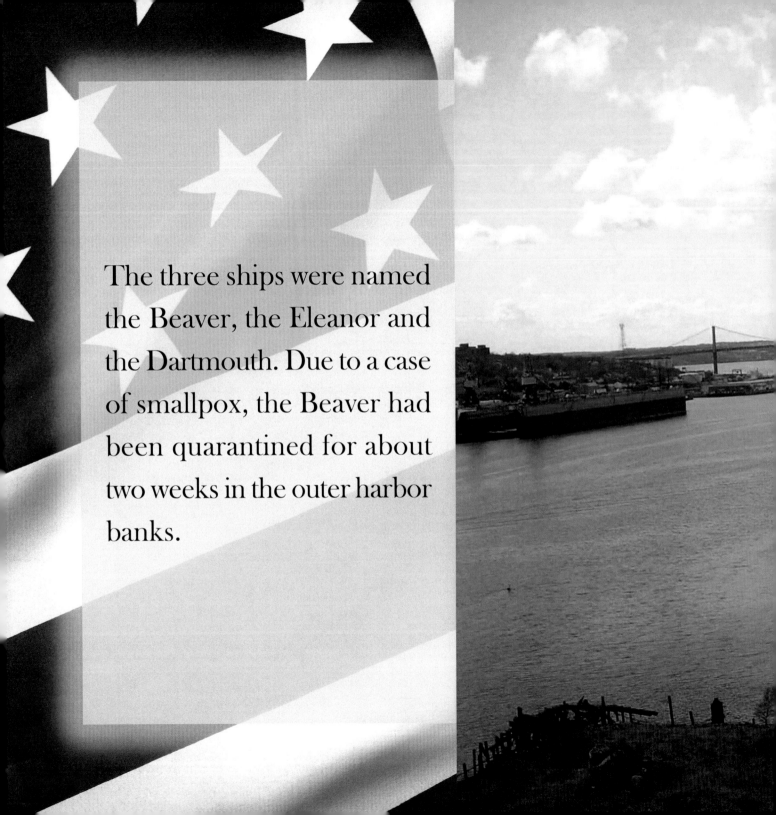

The three ships were named the Beaver, the Eleanor and the Dartmouth. Due to a case of smallpox, the Beaver had been quarantined for about two weeks in the outer harbor banks.

In all, 342 tea chests were tossed in the water. Some colonists wore Mohawk Indian costumes, but did not fool anybody. The British knew that the Colonists had tossed the tea into the ocean.

The Tea Trade Up To 1767

As they began to develop a liking for tea near the 17th century, companies began to import the tea from China. The British Parliament provided the East India Company the monopoly in 1698 to import the tea.

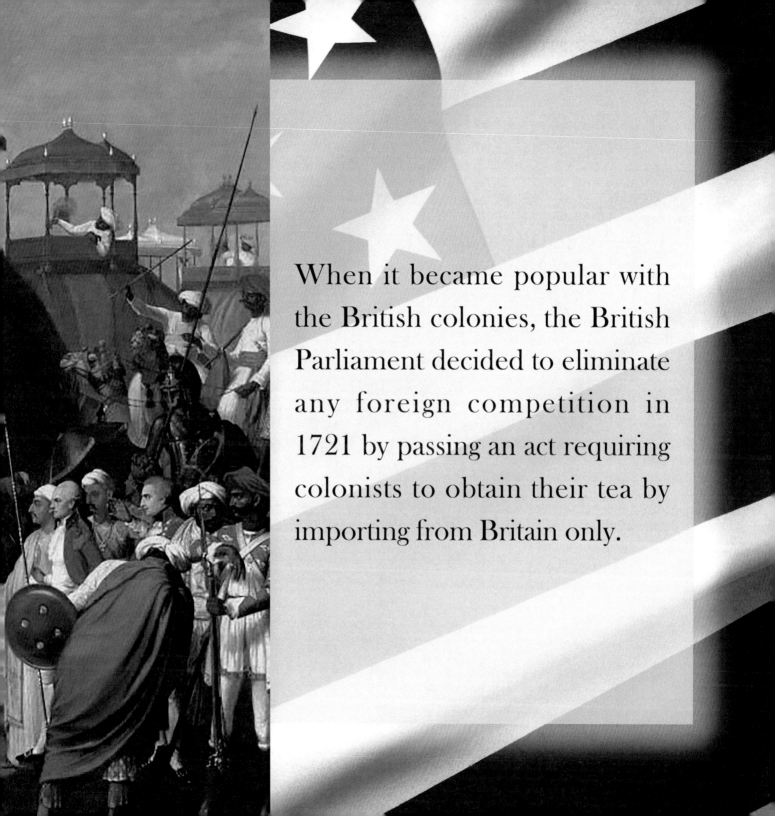

When it became popular with the British colonies, the British Parliament decided to eliminate any foreign competition in 1721 by passing an act requiring colonists to obtain their tea by importing from Britain only.

The East India Company was not able to export their tea, and could only wholesale it at English auctions. The British would buy the tea and export it to the American colonies, where it was resold to merchants in Charleston, New York, Boston and Philadelphia.

The East India Company would pay an ad valorem tax of approximately 25% until 1767. Parliament then laid additional taxes on the tea sold to be consumed in Britain. Combined with the fact that the tea that was imported to the Dutch Republic was not taxed by their government, these taxes meant that the British Americans and the Britons would be able to purchase smuggled Dutch tea at lower prices.

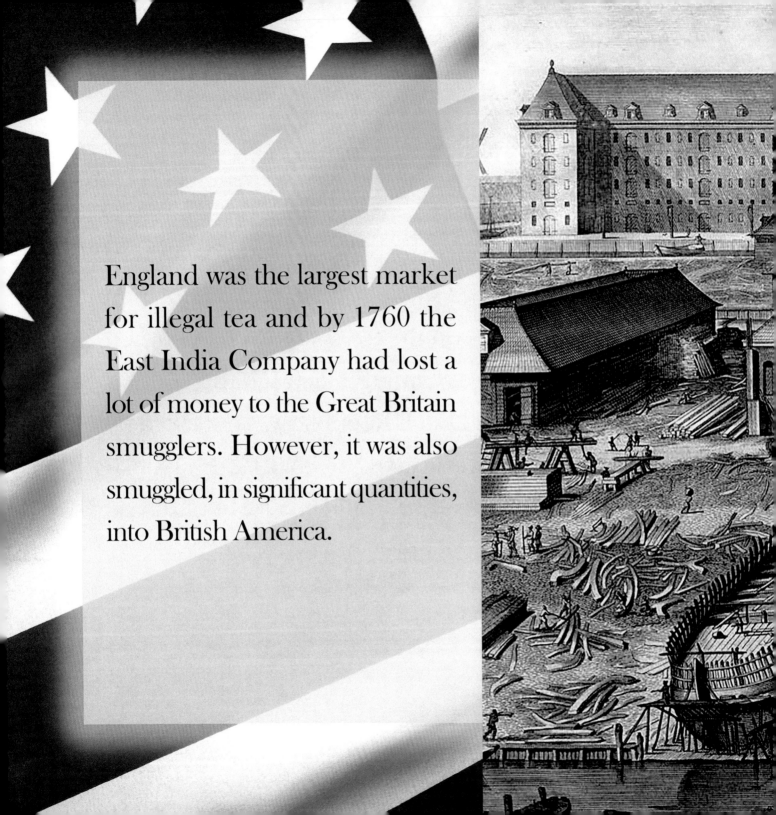

England was the largest market for illegal tea and by 1760 the East India Company had lost a lot of money to the Great Britain smugglers. However, it was also smuggled, in significant quantities, into British America.

To assist the East India Company to compete with the smuggled tea, in 1767 Parliament passed the Indemnity Act. This Act lowered taxes on tea consumed there and refunded the East India Tea Company a 25% duty that was then re-exported to the thirteen colonies. Parliament also then passed the Townshend Revenue Act of 1767 to help with this loss of revenue.

This act added new taxes, including one for the tea, within the American colonies. However, rather than solving the problem with smuggling, this Act merely renewed the controversy surrounding the right of Parliament to tax these colonies.

The Tea Act Of 1773

The Indemnity Act of 1767, refunding the duty on tea to the East India Company ended in 1772. In 1772, Parliament then passed another act that reduced the refund, lowering it to 10% duty on the tea Britain imported. It also restored the taxes on tea that had been repealed back in 1767. Since the new tax proceeded to drive up the cost of the tea, sales went down. While the company still imported tea into Great Britain, they were gaining a huge surplus of something that was not selling. By the latter part of 1772 the East India Company was in a severe financial catastrophe.

On May 10, 1773, King George assented to the Tea Act. This provided restoration to the East India Company and also allowed it to export the tea to the American Colonies by its own account. This allowed them to decrease their costs in eliminating the middleman who would purchase it at auctions in London. Rather than involving a middleman, they could now appoint colonial merchants to consign the tea. They could then sell it for a commission. The tea consignees were selected in July 1773 at locations in Charleston, Boston, Philadelphia and New York.

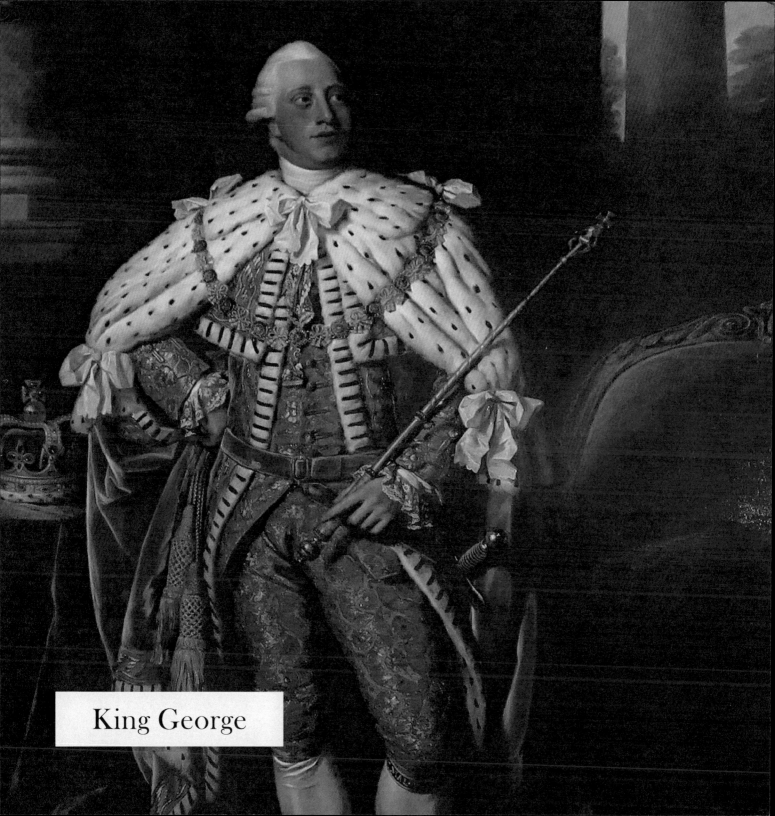

King George

Why Did They Do It?

In each of the colonies except Massachusetts, the protesters managed to force the consignees to either return the tea to England or resign. However, Governor Hutchison in Boston, became determined to stand his ground. He convinced the consignees not to back down, including two of them that were his sons.

When the ship Dartmouth arrived in late November, Whig leader, known as Samuel Adams, called for a meeting of the masses to be held November 29, 1773. Thousands arrived and the meeting had to be moved to the Old South Meeting House.

Samuel Adams

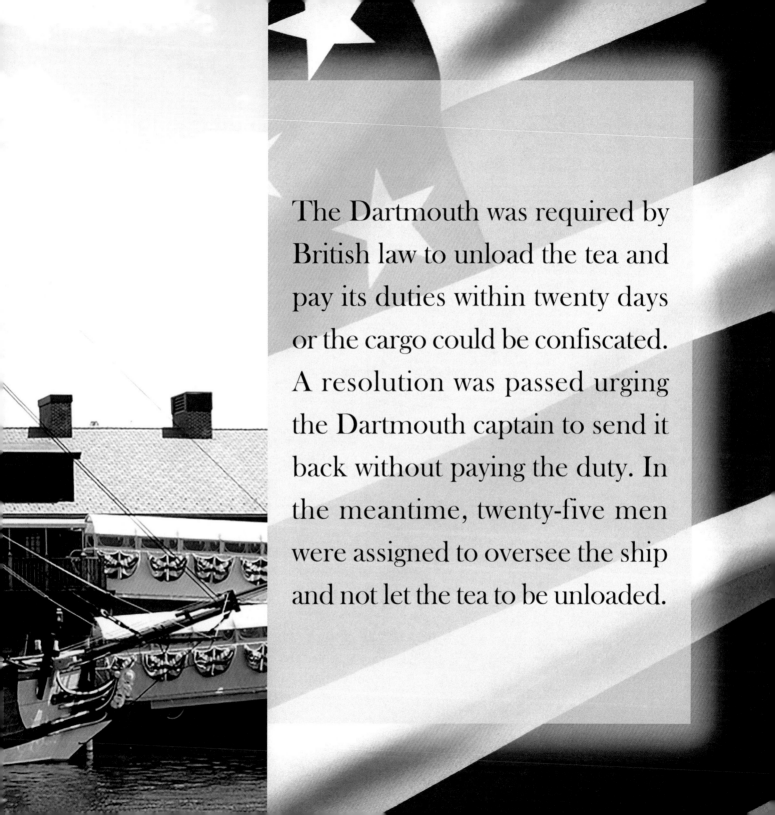

The Dartmouth was required by British law to unload the tea and pay its duties within twenty days or the cargo could be confiscated. A resolution was passed urging the Dartmouth captain to send it back without paying the duty. In the meantime, twenty-five men were assigned to oversee the ship and not let the tea to be unloaded.

Historians are unclear as to whether or not this protest was organized. Earlier that day a town meeting took place commanded by Samuel Adams, discussing these taxes and what to do about them. No one, however, is sure if Samuel Adams planned this tea destruction or if this was simply a group of people that got mad and went ahead with the destruction of the tea. Later, Sam Adams did indicate that it was a case of people defending their rights and not the act of an angry group of people.

Samuel Adams

Two more ships, the Beaver and the Eleanor, arrived to the harbor. On the last day of the deadline for the Dartmouth, December 16, around 7,000 people were at the Old South Meeting House. Once they received notice that the Governor had refused again to let these ships leave, Adams proceeded to state that "This meeting can do nothing further to save the Country".

It is believed that this was a signal that had been arranged previously to begin the "tea party". This claim, however, was not found in print for nearly a century in Adams' biography, written by his great-grandson, and he may have misinterpreted the evidence.

According to the accounts of eyewitnesses, no one started leaving for ten or fifteen minutes after this "alleged" signal and that Adams did try to stop people because the meeting wasn't over yet.

What's The Big Deal?

It was a lot of tea. There was 90,000 pounds of tea in the 342 containers that were tossed into the ocean. That would be worth about a million dollars in our money today.

The Boston Tea Party was significant in bringing about the American Revolution.

In 1774, Parliament responded with its Coercive Acts, also known as the Intolerable Acts, which ended the local self-governing in Massachusetts and closed the commerce for Boston.

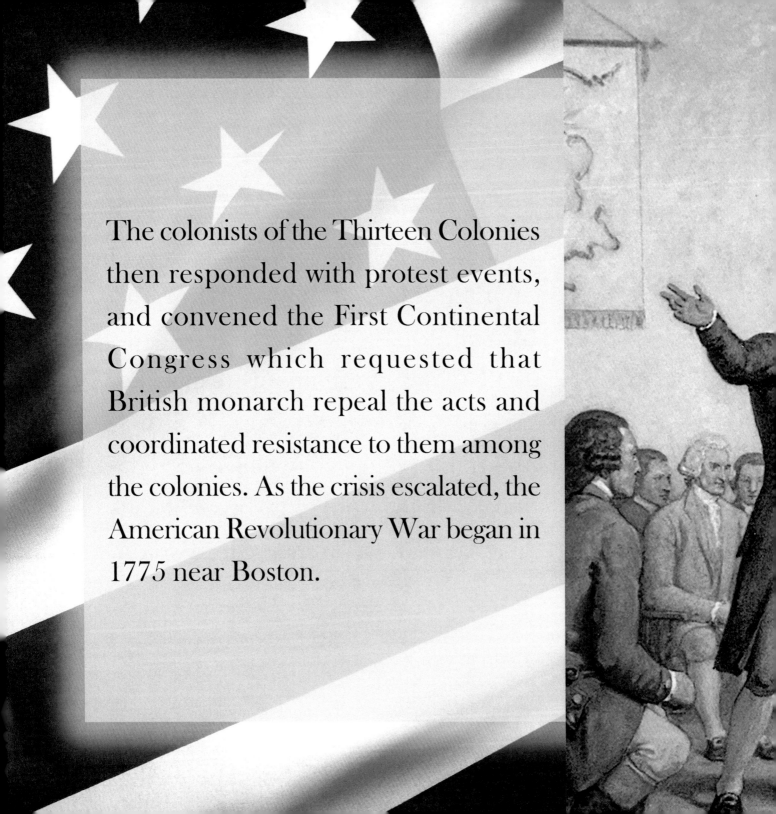

The colonists of the Thirteen Colonies then responded with protest events, and convened the First Continental Congress which requested that British monarch repeal the acts and coordinated resistance to them among the colonies. As the crisis escalated, the American Revolutionary War began in 1775 near Boston.

The First Continental Congress

The Intolerable Acts

These Acts were termed by the Patriots as laws passed as punishment in 1774 as a result of the Boston Tea Party. These laws were created as punishment for the colonists' act of defiance in throwing the tea into the water. They were known as the Coercive laws by Great Britain.

These acts triggered outrage as well as resistance from the Colonies by taking Massachusetts' historic and self-governing rights.

In 1775, they also presented key developments resulting in a movement in 1775 towards the American Revolution.

We the Lady's
of Edenton do
hereby Solemnly
Engage not to Conform
to that Pernicious Custom
of Drinking Tea, or that we the
aforesaid Lady's will not promote if wear
of any Manufacture from England
untill such time that all Acts
which tend to Enslave this our
Native Country shall be Repealed.

While four out the five acts were created in response to the Boston Tea Party, Parliament had hoped that these measures would reverse the resistance of the colonies to their authority created by the Stamp Act of 1765.

The Quebec Act then enlarged boundaries of Quebec and added modifications that favored the French Catholic people in the region. Even though it was not related to the four other acts, this act was passed at the same time and was seen as another Intolerable Act.

The Patriots saw this act as a violation of Massachusetts' rights and they then organized the First Continental Congress in 1774 in order to organize a protest. Once tensions began to escalate, the American Revolutionary War began in April of 1775, leading to the independence declaration of the United States in July of 1776.

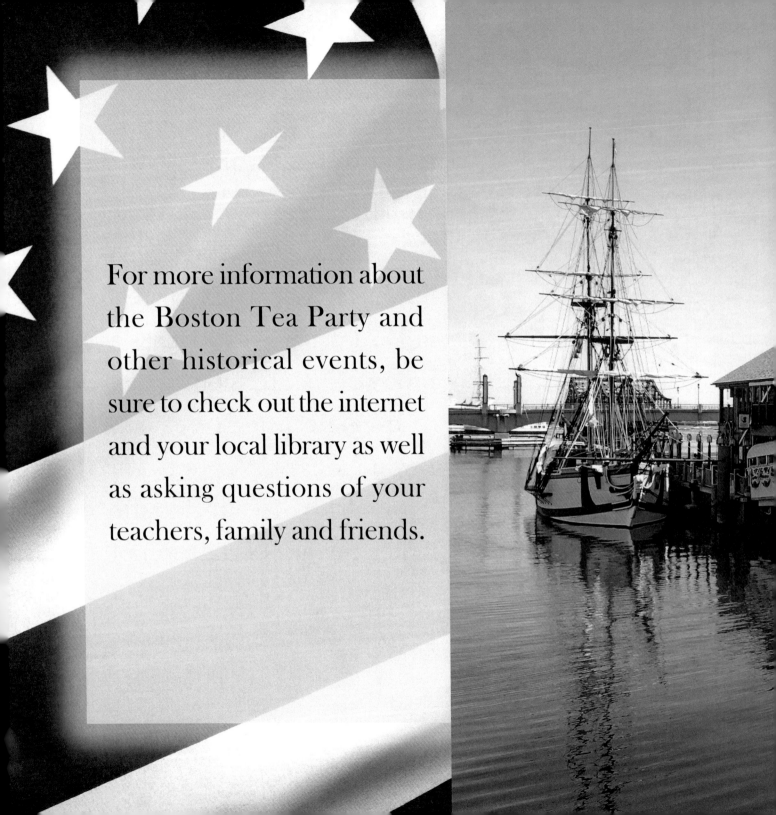

For more information about the Boston Tea Party and other historical events, be sure to check out the internet and your local library as well as asking questions of your teachers, family and friends.

Made in United States
North Haven, CT
14 March 2023